Deserts

Catherine Chambers

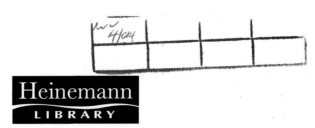

Heinemann LIBRARY

First published in Great Britain by Heinemann Library,
Halley Court, Jordan Hill, Oxford OX2 8EJ,
a division of Reed Educational and Professional Publishing Ltd.
Heinemann is a registered trademark of Reed Educational & Professional Publishing Limited.

OXFORD MELBOURNE AUCKLAND
JOHANNESBURG BLANTYRE GABORONE
IBADAN PORTSMOUTH NH (USA) CHICAGO

Designed by David Oakley
Illustrations by Tokay Interactive Ltd
Originated by Dot Gradations
Printed in Hong Kong/China

05 04 03 02 01
10 9 8 7 6 5 4 3 2 1

ISBN 0 431 09848 4
This title is also available in a hardback library edition (ISBN 0 431 09841 7)

British Library Cataloguing in Publication Data

Chambers, Catherine
    Deserts. – (Mapping earthforms)
    1. Desert ecology – Juvenile literature 2. Deserts – Maps –
    Juvenile literature
    I. Title
    577.5'4

Acknowledgements
The Publishers would like to thank the following for permission to reproduce photographs: Ecoscene: R Hughes p27; Robert Harding Picture Library: R Ashworth p25, J Greenberg p7; Anthony King: p15; Oxford Scientific Films: K Atkinson p9, M Brown p12, F Ehrenstrom p17, J Foote p18, C Monteath p19, R Packwood p11; G R Roberts: pp8, 10, 24; Still Pictures: p23, R Buttiker p26, M Denis-Hoot p13, W Fautre p5, S Pern p4, H Schwarzbach p22, UNEP p20, G Wiltsie p29.

Cover photograph reproduced with permission of Bruce Coleman Limited.

Every effort has been made to contact copyright holders of any material reproduced in this book. Any omissions will be rectified in subsequent printings if notice is given to the Publisher.

For more information about Heinemann Library books, or to order, please phone ++44 (0)1865 888066, or send a fax to ++44 (0)1865 314091. You can visit our website at www.heinemann.co.uk.

Any words appearing in the text in bold, **like this**, are explained in the Glossary.

Contents

What is a desert?   4

Deserts of the world   6

Desert landscapes   8

Shaped by the rain   10

Shaped by the wind   12

Water in the desert   14

Plants of the desert   16

Desert creatures   18

Peoples of the desert   20

The riches of the desert   22

A way of life – the Aborigines of Australia   24

Looking to the future   26

Desert facts   28

Glossary   30

Index   32

What is a desert?

Most deserts are huge areas of very dry land. Some deserts are frozen. All deserts are so dry or frozen that very few plants are able to grow in them. They receive less than 25 centimetres of rain each year – or even none at all.

There are hot, cold and frozen deserts. Deserts that lie on high **plateaux**, where the air is cooler, are called 'cold'. But they are, in fact, often very hot during the day. In the **polar regions**, deserts are frozen all year round. At night, hot, cold and frozen deserts are all very cold indeed.

How did deserts begin?

Some deserts began thousands of years ago. Others have existed for not much more than 1000 years. The hot **climate** in some

The Gobi is a cold desert that lies on a plateau in central Asia. It has rolling hills covered in small stones. Some deserts have a covering of volcanic gravel.

The Sahara is a hot desert that covers much of north Africa. Just over 8000 years ago, it was green and **fertile.** There are signs of ancient river valleys that once wound through what is now dry desert.

parts of the world dried up the earth. We will find out how today's climate keeps our deserts dry. We will also discover how humans are causing some deserts to spread.

What do deserts look like?

Some deserts are very rocky, while others are covered with stones or gravel. Some are vast stretches of fine sand, while others are huge areas of ice.

High winds and sudden showers of rain have made strange shapes out of the desert rocks and sand. We will discover how different types of desert are made and how the shapes are still being formed.

Life in the desert

Deserts look very bare. But plants and animals have found ways of living in them. Humans have made their homes in deserts too. We will find out how living things are able to survive in the deserts of the world. We will also see what the future holds for them.

Deserts of the world

Coastal deserts and cold, dry winds

All deserts lie in areas of the world where there is very little rain. Take a look at the world map below. You can see that all the deserts are on huge masses of land called **continents**. Many of the deserts lie on the western side of these continents. Here, it is dry because winds blowing from the west sweep across cold oceans. The coldness stops the air from holding the kind of moisture that forms rain clouds. So these western coasts remain dry.

Some deserts are cold or cool, even though they lie near the Equator. The Gobi Desert stretches along a high, flat **plateau.** The high **altitude** makes the air very cold. The Namib Desert in south-west Africa is cool because of a cold ocean **current** that runs along the coast. This chills the air above it, which gets blown on to the desert.

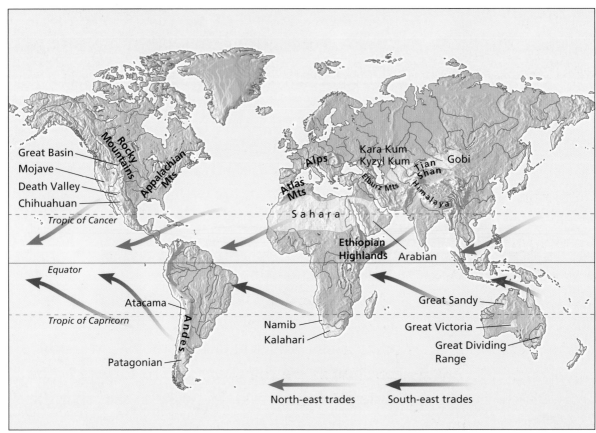

Dry rain-shadow areas

You will also see that some of the deserts lie to the west of huge mountain ranges. The Andes in South America, the Rockies in North America and the Great Dividing Range in Australia are examples of these ranges. The deserts to the west of them are sheltered from the constant winds that bring rain clouds. To the north of the **Equator**, these winds always blow towards the south-west. To the south of the Equator they blow towards the north-west. As these winds cross the mountain ranges they become colder and the **water vapour** in them cools and falls as rain. By the time the winds have crossed the mountain ranges the air is very dry.

Tropical deserts

The map also shows that many deserts lie up to 1500 kilometres north or south of the Equator. These areas are known as the **Tropics**. In parts of the Tropics, the skies are clear, with very few rain clouds. The hot sun beats down on the earth, drying it out. Tropical deserts have formed in these parts.

The Mojave Desert lies in California in the USA. It is sheltered all round by mountains and so gets very little rainfall. The desert is hot, but some of the surrounding mountain peaks are covered in snow.

7

Desert landscapes

Desert types

Deserts have many strangely shaped rocks and sand **dunes** that look like huge waves. But these are just some of the features that make up the three main types of desert landscape – rocky, sandy and stony. Rocky deserts are known as **hamada**. Sandy deserts are called **erg** and stony deserts are known as **reg**. These are Arabic names; Arabia itself has many desert types.

There are two main things that have made these desert varieties. The first is the type of rock from which different deserts are made. Some crystal-like rocks break down into sand. Harder rocks break down into stones or leave large pieces of rock on the landscape. Soft rocks wear down into hills and then into low-lying **plains**. The second thing that makes the desert types is the force of sudden rain and winds that **erode** the deserts.

◆ Hot deserts can have a thin, dark surface layer called 'desert varnish'. It is made from iron deposits. In many places there is also a fine crust of plant roots, known as a microfloral crust. Flowers burst from these plants when it rains. These top layers help to stop the wind from eroding the desert. They take thousands of years to form.

Weakened rocks

The most important factor in shaping the desert is water. It is not only important because it lashes down on rocks and sand. The chemicals in water weaken desert rock, so that it wears away more easily. Rain-water has **minerals** and **acids** in it which change the chemicals in the rocks, making them crumbly. Dew that forms on the rocks at night does this too. So does moisture that gets sucked up from the ground. This weakening action is known as chemical **weathering**.

Physical weathering processes then take over. In hot deserts, the sun's heat and the night's freezing temperatures weaken rocks and stones further. The sun beats down on them during the day. This makes them expand. At night the skies are clear and the ground lies unprotected by cloud. So cold, crisp air quickly cools the rocks and stones, making them shrink and crack. Any water that gathers in small cracks in the rock freezes at night. The water expands, gradually pushing the rocks further apart. Over time, these actions weaken the rocks along their natural joints. They are then very vulnerable to rainstorms and high winds.

What a strange sight! But this isn't a river in the sand. – it's only a **mirage**. Mirages form where layers of air at different temperatures meet, bending the rays of sunlight that beam down on them. In hot deserts the air near the ground becomes hotter than the air above it, causing a mirage.

Shaped by the rain

When rainstorms break over rocky deserts, flash floods hit the dry desert landscape. Water lashes down on the hard, bare surface. There is no soil to soak it up. There are no plants to protect the rock surface either. Raindrops batter bare rock and stones, wearing them away. Rain also collects in streams, called **rivulets**. These wear grooves, known as **gullies**. The rivulets also carry small, gritty particles with them, which scrape at the surface, making the gullies deeper.

When streams gather at the bottom of rocky hills they carve out gigantic **canyons** or **gorges**. These divide high, flat **plateaux**. Single rocks can get separated from the plateau by the gorge. These are called **inselbergs**. Some are flat-topped rocks called **mesas**. Others are small pointed rocks, known as **buttes**. After a long time, soft rocks can get worn down into a low-lying **plain**. There is sometimes a shallow slope at the bottom of cliffs, where the cliffs meet the plain.

◈ Monument Valley in the USA is a spectacular desert landscape. Its amazing shapes have mostly been made by water **erosion**. In parts, there are humped cone hills as far as the eye can see. There are ridges, gullies, canyons and **spires** too. This dry desert landscape is made of layers of soft, **sedimentary** rock. When this rock is eroded by rainstorms, the layers help to make these unusual shapes. Rain also exposes the different colours of the layers.

The Great Fish River lies in south-west Africa. It is normally dry but when there is sudden rain, the wadi is filled with water. The river is then 100 m wide and 9 m deep.

Rivers in the sand

Heavy rain makes sudden rivers that cut deeply into sandy and stony deserts. The water carries sand or gravel with it, which **scour** the river beds making them deeper. The rain stops and the rivers quickly dry up. Dry river beds, called **wadis**, are left. But it is thought that many of the wadis in the Sahara and Arabian Deserts actually began when the **climate** was a lot wetter. So these were originally normal river beds.

The levels of rainfall at Eismitte, in Greenland, and Bahrain, on the edge of the Arabian Desert, are very similar, but the temperatures are very different.

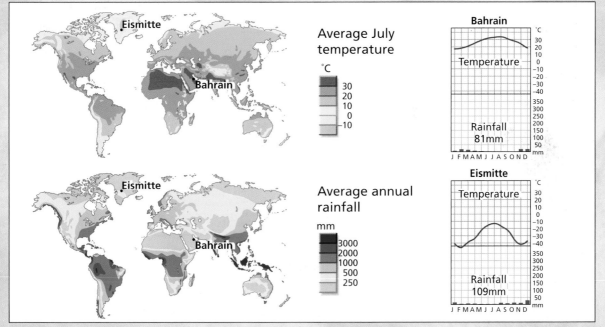

Eismitte

Average July temperature

°C

30
20
10
0
-10

Bahrain

Average annual rainfall

mm

3000
2000
1000
500
250

Bahrain

°C
30
20
10
0
-10
-20
-30
-40

Temperature

350
300
250
200
150
100
50
mm

Rainfall
81mm

J F M A M J J A S O N D

Eismitte

°C
30
20
10
0
-10
-20
-30
-40

Temperature

350
300
250
200
150
100
50
mm

Rainfall
109mm

J F M A M J J A S O N D

Shaped by the wind

Desert landscapes are also shaped by fierce desert winds. These bring small particles of sand and stone with them. They bounce along the ground and hit solid rocks, chipping and wearing them away. This type of **erosion** is called **abrasion**.

The wind and sand can wear away at the bottom of tall rocks, making mushroom shapes called **pedestals**. They can make ridges and furrows in the rock, known as **yardangs** and **zeugens**. Or they can make flat rock surfaces with sharp edges. Sand carried in the wind polishes these rock faces, making them smooth and shiny.

All these wind-blown shapes are really quite small. Most of the big features, such as **plains** and **plateaux,** were made by rain. But there is one very large feature that is

The Rub al-Khali in Arabia is one of the hottest sandy deserts of the world. It is also known as the Empty Quarter because it is so hard for living things to survive there. The desert covers about 650,000 sq km (250,000 sq mi) and is linked to other sandy and rocky deserts in the region. Some of the massive dunes in Rub al-Khali are so old that the sand in them has hardened into sandstone. The pattern of stone layers shows how the wind blew the sand in one direction.

12

eroded by wind. This is the deflation hollow, which is a huge, **scoured**-out **basin**. The rock was probably first weakened and crumbled by chemical **weathering** (see page 9). The wind then blew away the fragile surface. The Qattara Depression is a deflation hollow that lies in western Egypt. It lies about 130 metres below sea level and is hundreds of kilometres wide.

Heaps of sand

Winds also blow sandy deserts into **dunes**. Some are peaks as high as 200 metres. Others are shaped by the wind into **crescents**, called **barchans**, and **seifs**, which are snake-like. These formations are caused by a strong wind blowing in just one direction. The sand in the dunes is pushed over and around the shapes by the wind. This makes the shapes move across the desert. Star shapes are formed when the wind swirls in different directions.

In Saudi Arabia, sand dunes move at an average of 14.6 metres each year. They clog pipelines that carry petroleum oil from oil wells to the country's **refineries**. Barriers have been built and trees have been planted to try and stop this. In the Antarctic, the cold winds sweep snow and ice into deep drifts that look like dunes.

◈ Pedestal formations like this one occur because their rocks lie in **horizontal** soft and hard layers of rock. Wind erosion wears away the soft layer, leaving the shape of the hard layer towering above the ground. Yardangs and zeugens form in the same way.

Water in the desert

Without water, there would be no spectacular desert landscapes. But most importantly, without water there would be no life in the deserts at all. Water in the desert comes in three main forms. It comes as night dew that clings to rocks and stones, as moisture that gets sucked up from the ground or as rare torrents of rain. Sometimes there are very light rain showers as well.

Running rivers and cool oases

Sudden rain in the desert causes rivers to flow for a short while along normally dry river beds. Sometimes, the rain causes flooding, bringing life to the desert.

Some oases are natural. The water rises at the point where hard, impermeable rocks curve up towards the surface of the desert. Other oases are artificial. They were made by drilling down to the water table, making wells. Some wells are more than 1000 m deep. Although there are large cities along the north African coast, settlements in the Sahara Desert are sparse and based around oases.

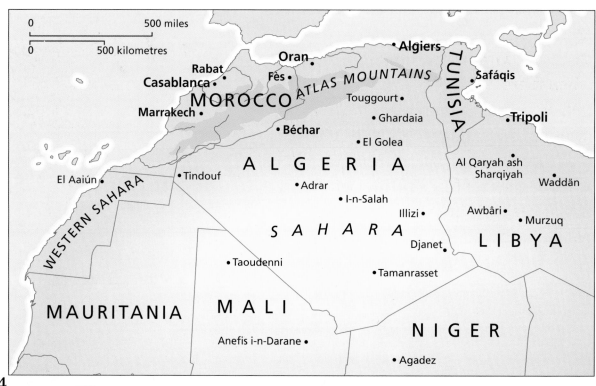

In some deserts, rain runs down mountain ranges, like the Atlas Range in the Sahara. This water flows underground. Sometimes, these underground rivers rise to the surface, making cool, damp areas known as **oases**.

At other times, the water collects underground between layers of **impermeable** rock, shaped in a **basin**. Impermeable means that water cannot soak through. The water rests in these basins forming underground lakes, known as artesian basins. When wells are drilled through the top layer of rock, the pressure is so great that the water spurts up.

Salt lakes – playas

Swift-flowing torrents of rain can carry **eroded** rocks and stones along with them. Some desert rocks contain salt **minerals**. When the rivers stop, the rocks and stones are dumped. These form rocky slopes called **bajadas**. The slopes get eroded into basins, which fill with water when there is sudden rain. When this lake dries up, the surface is covered with a glistening layer of salt, which has been drawn out of the rocks.

Palms and crops grow well in shady, damp oases like this one in Morocco.

Plants of the desert

Coping in the desert

Plants in the world's deserts have to cope with dry conditions and rapid changes in temperature. Some plants have adapted themselves over thousands of years to survive. Other plants only come to life when rain finally falls on the bare rocks and sand. In hot deserts, dry seeds can lie for years near the desert surface. When rain finally comes, a carpet of flowers covers the landscape.

Some plants have adapted to the high levels of salt and other chemicals often found in desert rock and sand. These plants are called **halophytes**. The salt is concentrated in the plant's sap and comes out through tiny holes in the leaves.

You can see from the map that the Sahara is fringed with grasslands to the south. Some deserts have no grasslands around their edges. Often there are only rocky mountains or the sea.

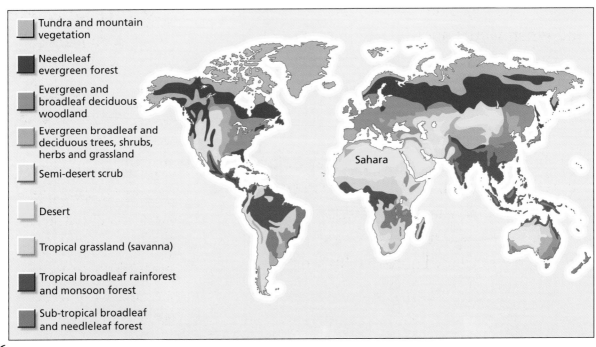

Tundra and mountain vegetation

Needleleaf evergreen forest

Evergreen and broadleaf deciduous woodland

Evergreen broadleaf and deciduous trees, shrubs, herbs and grassland

Semi-desert scrub

Desert

Tropical grassland (savanna)

Tropical broadleaf rainforest and monsoon forest

Sub-tropical broadleaf and needleleaf forest

Sahara

In Antarctica, there are no flowering plants at all. In the short summer, tiny mosses and **fungi** cling to small patches of bare rock. Lichens, which are a mixture of **algae** and fungi, spread a carpet of colour over the rocks too. Plants in freezing **climates** cannot suck up water through their roots, just like plants in hot deserts. This is because the water is frozen into ice.

Waxy cactus

The cactus grows mostly in the deserts of North and South America. Most have swollen stems with a waxy covering. This helps them to store water for a long time. The stems are shaped so that, when water does flow, it goes directly to the roots. The huge root system spreads out far and wide. This helps the plant to absorb as much water as possible.

Some cacti have sharp spines. These in fact are leaves. The spiny shape helps to stop the sun and heat from drying them out. It also stops animals from eating the cactus! Some cacti produce brilliant flowers and soft, fleshy fruit.

The opuntia cactus comes from Central America but is grown in many other dry regions of the world. It is used as a hedge to protect homes and animals such as sheep. It also shelters small patches of earth where crops are grown. The opuntia is also known as prickly pear because of its delicious, yellow, pear-shaped fruit. But in Australia the opuntia has grown so well that it has become a huge, prickly weed. Millions of dollars are spent trying to get rid of it.

17

Desert creatures

Adapting to the desert

A lot of desert **mammals** shelter from the heat of the day. They are nocturnal, which means they only come out of their burrows at night when it is cool. Small mammals such as the North American kangaroo rat and the African gerbil are able to hold water in their bodies and **recycle** it. They survive by eating dry seeds. Other animals, like the horned toad, can cool their bodies by controlling their heartbeat, making it pump more slowly.

Some **reptiles** and **amphibians** sleep, or **estivate**, during very dry periods. Amphibians like the Arizona spadefoot toad bury themselves deep in the earth until it rains. Then they scramble to the surface and quickly lay their **spawn** in the puddles that have formed. The puddles soon dry out but the young toads grow very quickly and then bury themselves underground, just like their parents.

There are no animals on the freezing land of the Antarctic – apart from some tiny flies. But the coasts are teeming with tiny plants and sea creatures, fish, seals and seabirds such as penguins. Their bodies have layers of fat which help them to cope with the energy they lose in the cold.

Arizona, USA, is the home of the roadrunner, a bird that sprints across the dry landscape to catch its prey of lizards and snakes. These give the roadrunner enough food and liquid to survive.

18

The camel – the ship of the desert

Camels are found in both hot and cold deserts.
The one-humped camel comes from hot Arabia.
The two-humped Bactrian camel comes from
cool central Asia. Camels can travel long
distances without food or water. So, for
hundreds of years, desert peoples and traders
have used camels to carry them, their goods
and even their homes.

The camel's hump stores fat and flesh, which the
body uses when food is scarce. A camel drinks a
huge amount of water when it can, but it
survives for several days without taking any
more. Water is stored in stomach pouches and
released into the body when needed.

Hard, **cloven** feet help the Bactrian camel to grip the rocks of central Asia's deserts. Its long hair keeps out the cold.

Peoples of the desert

Surviving in the desert

Some desert peoples have survived for thousands of years by collecting enough food and water to live, without disturbing the desert. They have found skilful ways of building shelters from the few bushes and trees that grow. Some make homes from hollows in cool desert-mountain cliffs. The San of southern Africa, the Tuareg of north and west Africa and the Aborigines of Australia live comfortably in this way. They have also developed rich cultures that have stemmed from their environment.

The Bedouin of Arabia and north Africa load camels with food, water and materials for housing. They herd sheep and goats, which provide meat, milk and wool. The wool is woven into tent material and clothing. Camel, goat and sheep's milk is made into cheese, or it is salted to keep it fresh.

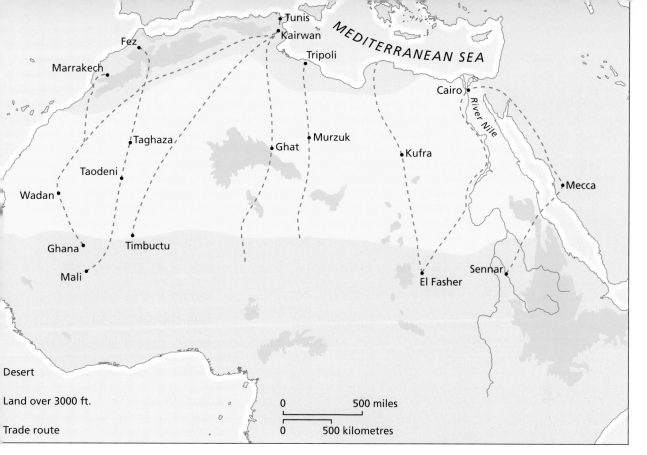

Desert

Land over 3000 ft.

Trade route

0   500 miles

0   500 kilometres

Growing food

In Saharan **oases**, cereals, fruit, vegetables and date palms are grown. Many of these foods are dried so that they keep for a long time. This is important for people who live and travel in the desert.

For thousands of years, farmers have grown food and cotton along the banks of the River Nile in the eastern Sahara. When the Nile flooded each year, it brought down rich river soils in which to grow crops. But these no longer **fertilize** the valley. This is because the Aswan **Dam** collects much of the Nile's water and allows only a small amount to flow down into the river. The rich, red soils now heap up behind the dam. In the cold deserts of Peru, farmers have used mountain streams to **irrigate** the dry land for many centuries.

Most desert peoples trade animals and other goods such as **minerals** and tools. Ancient trade routes have crossed the Sahara from the coasts of north Africa right down to the tropical forests of west Africa. Salt was an important trade item. People cannot survive in the heat without salt. Traders loaded camels with silks and gems along the Silk Road from China to Europe. This route cut across the cold, rocky deserts of central Asia.

The riches of the desert

Deserts hold many riches. Some, such as precious stones and gold, are mined from desert rock. Petroleum oil is extracted deep down in the ground. In the last century, these riches have been taken from the deserts and sold throughout the world. This has made some desert countries very wealthy. It has also given people work.

In other countries, water has been brought into the desert to make farmland. **Irrigation** channels have been made and deep wells have been dug. In the **Middle East**, some of the water has been used to make golf courses. This has encouraged tourists to visit the area.

This long canal runs for 680 km (423 mi) through the Thar Desert in north-west India. It was built so that huge areas of desert could become farmland. Here rice and other cereals, cotton, groundnuts and oilseeds are grown. But growing crops on reclaimed deserts has its problems. The earth dries out quickly, often leaving a crusty layer of salt on the top, which stops plants from growing.

Science in the desert

Antarctica is rich in **minerals**, especially oil and coal. But Antarctica is also one of the few remaining undisturbed **habitats** of the world. So the countries of the world have agreed only to use Antarctica to set up a research station. To protect the environment, only about 1000 scientists are allowed to live and work in Antarctica at any one time.

Oil and opals

Saudi Arabia is made up mostly of desert. Here, oil wells provide about a quarter of the world's petroleum oil every year. Underground pipelines carry oil from the oilfields to **refineries**.

Many different coloured **opals** are found in South Australia. In the desert mining town of Coober Pedy miners have made comfortable homes out of cool, empty mine holes dug into the rock.

Hot and cold deserts have a lot of sunshine. In California, a huge solar power station traps the sun's rays and changes them into electric energy. In California, too, farmers are using solar power to pump water on to their land. They are also adapting solar energy to create good growing environments in greenhouses.

A way of life – the Aborigines of Australia

Many parts of Australian deserts are semi-arid. This means that it is hot and dry for most of the time. At other times there is just enough rain for grasses, bushes and thin, spindly trees to grow. Some lizards, kangaroos, wild camels and birds are able to survive here. But for humans, it is very hard indeed. Aboriginal peoples of these deserts have learned many difficult skills which help them to live. They use the natural world to make a living and build a home.

Some desert homes are made from poles tied in a dome shape. They are covered with bundles of spinifex grass. Others have straight poles with a tree-bark roof. The bed is also made of poles and is raised above the ground. A fire is lit underneath to keep mosquitoes away.

Finding water

When Aborigines look at the landscape, they know the places where underground water lies. They dig a deep hole and muddy water is left to seep into it. A bunch of spinifex grass is then laid on top of the water. The grass gets soaked and is squeezed. Spinifex grass acts as a filter to make the water clear and pure.

Some trees have thick, juicy roots. These are dug up and scraped with a flat blade. The stringy fibres are then squeezed and water drips out.

Finding food

Some grass seeds, bush and tree roots and berries are gathered for food. Juicy grubs and caterpillars are also eaten. Birds, kangaroos and lizards are hunted. Guns and spears are used to hunt animals. The stringy **sinews** from animals' and birds' legs are used to tie poisoned arrowheads on to the spears.

Sometimes, food is cooked on hot stones. These are placed in a hole and covered with branches.

This picture is painted on rock and tells a traditional story. Aborigines learn desert routes through ancient songs and stories called songlines. Many of these are about animals and tell how the land was created. But they are also like maps. They tell where food and water can be found.

Looking to the future

Many of the world's deserts are growing bigger. This is known as desertification. It is caused by changes in **climate** and by human activity. In 1984, the **United Nations** made a study of desertification. It showed that, if we are not careful, nearly a third of the Earth's land could change into desert.

A hotter world

The world is getting slightly hotter all the time. This is called global warming. The thinning of a layer of gases high up in the Earth's atmosphere is partly to blame. This ozone layer stops harmful sun's rays from reaching the Earth. When it is too thin, the temperature on Earth rises. It is possible that the ozone layer is thinned by too many CFC gases in the atmosphere. CFC gases are found in aerosol cans and old

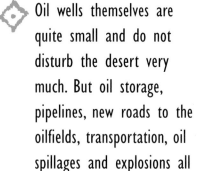
Oil wells themselves are quite small and do not disturb the desert very much. But oil storage, pipelines, new roads to the oilfields, transportation, oil spillages and explosions all harm the delicate desert environment.

refrigerators. But it is thought that flares from the Sun are making our Earth hotter too. The position of our Solar System as it moves around the galaxy is also making the Earth warmer.

Delicate deserts

Hot deserts have a thin, delicate, crusty surface. Roadbuilding, mining, farming and tourism break this fragile layer. So too does warfare. The desert environment of Kuwait was harmed by the Gulf War of 1991. Rolling tanks and burning oilfields destroyed the desert crust and created **sandstorms** in Arabia.

Desert plants are special because they have adapted themselves to the dry conditions. Sometimes farmers burn plants on the edges of deserts so that they can grow crops. Other farmers let their animals graze on them. In the end this makes the desert spread because there are no natural plants left to hold the soil together. An example of this is the Sahel region, on the edges of the Sahara.

Desert farms often use underground water from wells. This lowers the water table deep beneath the desert, which dries the desert even more. When underground desert water dries out on the farmland it often leaves high levels of salt and other chemicals.

Desert facts

Top ten desert regions

These are the biggest deserts in the world. Some of the regions are made up of several smaller deserts. This list does not include the frozen deserts in the **polar regions**.

	Location	**Area**
Sahara Desert	north Africa	8,600,000 sq km (3,320,000 sq mi)
Arabian Desert	south-west Asia	2,330,000 sq km (900,000 sq mi)
Gobi Desert	central Asia	1,300,000 sq km (500,000 sq mi)
Kalahari Desert	southern Africa	930,000 sq km (360,000 sq mi)
Patagonian Desert	Argentina	673,000 sq km (260,000 sq mi)
Great Victoria Desert	Australia	647,000 sq km (250,000 sq mi)
Great Basin	south-west USA	492,000 sq km (190,000 sq mi)
Chihuahuan Desert	Mexico	450,000 sq km (175,000 sq mi)
Great Sandy Desert	north-west Australia	400,000 sq km (150,000 sq mi)
Kara Kum Desert	Turkmenistan	350,000 sq km (135,000 sq mi)

Did you know that it can snow in hot deserts! It rarely happens, though. Snow falls when unusually strong winds blow very high up over the desert, where it is extremely cold. The moisture in the air freezes and falls as snow.

Years without rain

The driest place in the world is Arica, in Chile, which has an average of 0.8 mm of rain every year. The longest period without rain was also in Chile, at Calama, where there was no recorded rainfall at all until it rained in 1971.

Death Valley is a dry, often salty desert in south-east California and Nevada. It has the highest recorded temperature in the USA — 56.7°Celsius. Death Valley is famous for its rich borax deposits which were first mined over 100 years ago. Borax is used in glass-making and as a disinfectant.

Glossary

abrasion erosion caused by moving stones carried by wind or water

acid chemical substance that can corrode or damage other materials

algae simple form of plant life, ranging from a single cell to a huge seaweed

altitude height above sea level

amphibian animal, with a backbone, that develops in water and can stay in the water for long periods, but can also live on land. Frogs, toads and newts are amphibians.

bajada rocky slope formed from stones deposited by running water

barchan crescent-shaped sand dune

basin large hollow in the land, which slopes downwards like the inside of a washbasin, often with a river at the bottom

butte pointed rock separated from a rock mass by erosion

canyon narrow, steep-sided river valley

climate rainfall, temperature and winds that normally affect a large area

cloven hoof which is divided – sheep and oxen have cloven hooves

continent the world's largest land masses. Continents are usually divided into many countries.

crescent curved shape, like a new moon

current strong surge of water that flows constantly in one direction in an ocean

dam wall that is built across a river valley to hold back water, creating an artificial lake

dune huge heap of sand formed by the wind, which looks like a wave

Equator imaginary line around the Earth, exactly half way between the North and South Poles

erg sandy desert landscape

erosion wearing away of rocks and soil by wind, water, ice or acid

estivate sleep during very hot periods

fertile rich soil in which crops can grow easily. If you fertilize something you make it fertile.

fungus simple plant, such as a mould, mushroom or toadstool

gorge narrow river valley with very steep sides

gully groove worn into rock by rivulets

habitat place where a plant or animal usually grows or lives

halophyte plant that can cope with salty growing conditions

hamada rocky desert landscape

horizontal in line with the ground or the horizon

impermeable substance that does not allow water to pass through it

inselberg rock separated from a desert mountain or plateau by erosion

irrigate supply a place or area with water, for example to grow crops

mammal animal that feeds its young with its own milk

mesa flat-topped rock separated from a plateau by erosion

Middle East area between the eastern Mediterranean and India, particularly Israel and the Arab countries

mineral substance that is formed naturally in rock or earth, such as oil or salt

mirage optical illusion caused by light being bent through layers of warm air near the ground

oasis area of wet, fertile land in the middle of a desert

opal whitish gem with streaks of colour in it

pedestal mushroom-shaped rock shaped by wind erosion

plain area of flat land or low-lying hills

plateau area of high, flat ground, often lying between mountains

polar region area around the North and South Poles

recycle reuse

refinery factory where a raw substance, such as oil, is changed into one that can be more easily used

reg stony desert landscape

reptile cold-blooded, egg-laying animal with a spine and a scaly skin, such as a crocodile

rivulet stream that runs across rocks

sandstorm desert storm where the wind picks up clouds of sand

scour rub hard against something, wearing it away

sedimentary relatively soft type of rock formed by squashing eroded soil and deposits over millions of years

seif long, narrow sand dune

sinew strong, stringy substance that joins a muscle to a bone

spawn egg cells produced by some animals

spire something that is very tall, thin and pointed at the top

Tropics the region between the Tropic of Cancer and the Tropic of Capricorn. These are two imaginary lines drawn around the Earth, above and below the Equator.

United Nations world-wide organization set up to deal with problems facing the Earth and all living things in it

wadi dry river bed

water vapour water that has been heated so much that it forms a gas which is held in the air – drops of water form again when the vapour is cooled. There is always water vapour present in the air.

weathering action of weather on rock or other materials

yardang ridge formed by wind erosion

zeugen flat-topped ridge formed by wind erosion

Index

Aborigines 20, 24, 25

abrasion 12

acids 9

algae 17

Andes Mountains 7

Antarctica 13, 17, 18, 23

Arabian Desert 8, 11, 28

Aswan Dam, Egypt 21

Australia 7, 17, 23, 24, 25, 28

Bahrain 11

bajadas 15

barchan dune 13

Bedouin 20

borax 29

buttes 10

cacti 17

camels 19, 20

CFC gases 26

chemical weathering 9, 13

Chihuahuan Desert, Mexico 28

Chile 29

climate 4, 5, 6, 7, 11, 17, 26, 28

Death Valley, USA 29

deflation hollows 13

desert varnish 8

dunes 8, 12, 13

Eismitte, Greenland 11

Equator 6, 7

erg desert 8

erosion 5, 8, 10, 12, 13, 15

flash floods 10

fungi 17

Gobi Desert 4, 6, 28

gorges 10

Great Basin, USA 28

Great Dividing Range,
    Australia 7

Great Fish River 11

Great Sandy Desert,
    Australia 28

Great Victoria Desert,
    Australia 28

Gulf War 27

halophytes 16

hamada desert 8

India 22

inselbergs 10

irrigation 22

Kalahari Desert 28

Kara Kum Desert,
    Turkmenistan 28

Kuwait 27

mesas 10

minerals 9, 15, 21

mirages 9

Mojave Desert, USA 7

Monument Valley, USA 10

Morocco 15

Namib Desert 6

Nile, River 21

oil 13, 23, 26

opals 23

opuntia cactus (prickly pear) 17

Patagonian Desert,
    Argentina 28

pedestals 12, 13

Peru 21

plateaux 4, 6, 10, 12

polar regions 4, 28

Qattara Depression 13

rainfall 4, 5, 6, 9, 10, 11, 14, 24, 28

reg desert 8

rivers 5, 11, 14

roadrunners 18

Rocky Mountains 7

Rub al-Khali
    (Empty Quarter) 12

Sahara Desert 5, 11, 14, 16, 21,
    27, 28

salt 15, 16, 21, 22

salt lakes 15

sandstorms 27

San people 20

Saudi Arabia 13, 23

sedimentary rock 10

seif dune 13

solar power 23

songlines 25

spinifex grass 25

spires 10

Thar Desert 22

Tropics 7

Tuareg people 20

United Nations 26

USA 7, 10, 18, 23, 28, 29

vegetation 16, 17, 24

wadis 11

weathering 9

winds 6, 7, 12, 13

yardangs 12, 13

zeugens 12, 13